LOOK-AND-FIND
EASTER STORIES
FOR YOUNG CHILDREN

ILLUSTRATED BY
MEGAN HIGGINS

WHO WAS JESUS?

Jesus was God's son. Many people followed him, learning all about God's love through Jesus's teachings and amazing miracles. He prayed over a boy's lunch, and it became enough to feed more than five thousand people! He walked on water! He even raised a girl from the dead! Jesus showed us how to welcome and include everyone—because we are all important to God.

LOOK-AND-FIND

1 one teaching Jesus

2 two pairs of hugging friends

3 three listening critters

4 four notetaker's scrolls

5 five tree climbers

6 six blue sashes

7 seven lost sandals

8 eight purple figs

9 nine hilltop buildings

10 ten blossoming bushes

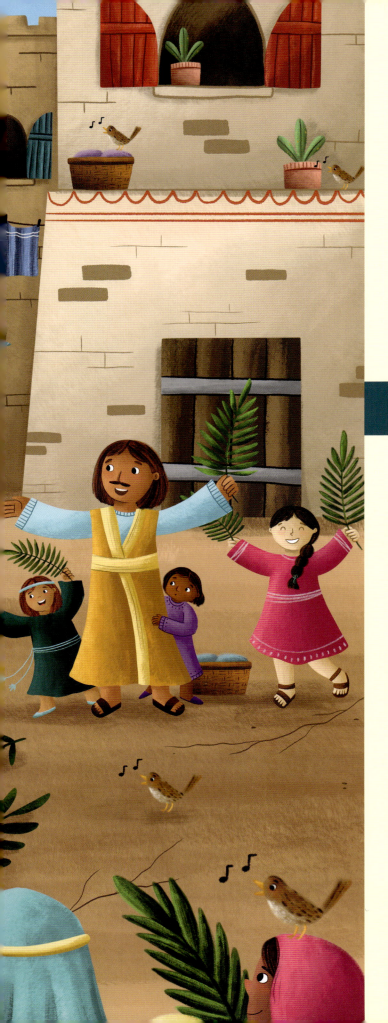

PALM PARADE

Many people admired Jesus. When the city of Jerusalem was full of people celebrating Passover, Jesus rode in on a donkey. A large crowd of people cheered and waved palm branches in greeting. They shouted, "Hosanna!" Christians remember this day on Palm Sunday!

LOOK-AND-FIND

1 one tired donkey

2 two shy children

3 three purple slashes

4 four long braids

5 five crooked cracks

6 six sun rays

7 seven woven baskets

8 eight houseplants

9 nine singing larks

10 ten waving palms

THE LAST SUPPER

Jesus loved everyone, but he knew that not everyone liked him very much. Although many people had welcomed him into town, others didn't like how popular Jesus had become.

When Jesus celebrated Passover with his disciples, he knew that it would be the last time. Jesus gave thanks for the bread and then broke it, saying, "This is my body. Take and eat. Do this to remember me." Then, Jesus took a cup, gave thanks, and said, "Drink from this cup. It is my blood, poured out in forgiveness."

LOOK-AND-FIND

1 one piece of broken bread

2 two painted vases

3 three open windows

4 four full jugs

5 five pairs of folded hands

6 six empty plates

7 seven hairy beards

8 eight loaves of bread

9 nine lit candles

10 ten cups of wine

PRAYING IN THE GARDEN

After dinner, Jesus and a few disciples went to pray in a garden called Gethsemane. Jesus knew his life was in danger. He asked the disciples to pray for him, but they kept falling asleep! Jesus prayed and asked God to help him. Jesus said, "Father, may your will be done."

But not all the disciples were there to pray. One, named Judas, brought soldiers to the garden. Judas told them who Jesus was, and they arrested him.

LOOK-AND-FIND

1 one spying Judas

2 two blooming bushes

3 three sleeping disciples

4 four fruit trees

5 five sly foxes

6 six palm plants

7 seven bunches of grapes

8 eight watchful birds

9 nine broken branches

10 ten shining stars

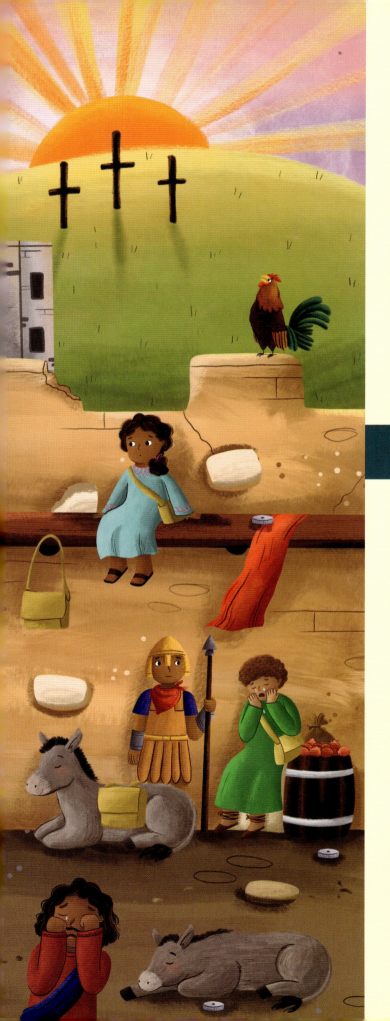

JESUS DIES

Peter, one of the disciples, followed behind Jesus and the soldiers. Someone in the crowd asked Peter if he knew Jesus, but he denied it. When another asked, he said no again. Later, a third person asked, and Peter said, "I do not know who you were talking about!" Just then, a rooster crowed.

Peter wept, and the soldiers took Jesus away. They nailed Jesus to a cross, and he died there.

LOOK-AND-FIND

1 one crowing rooster

2 two crying disciples

3 three curious people

4 four snoozing donkeys

5 five full barrels

6 six Roman soldiers

7 seven red scarves

8 eight heavy handbags

9 nine large stones

10 ten silver coins

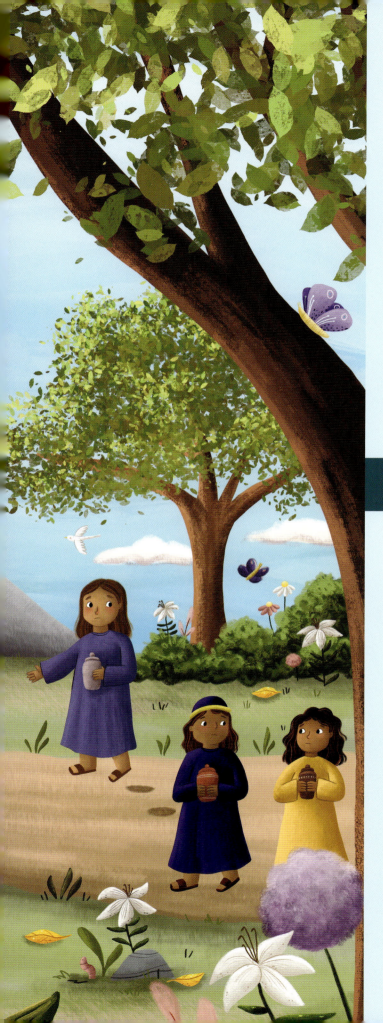

THE EMPTY TOMB

Three days after Jesus died, Mary Magdalene, Joanna, and Mary the mother of James visited the tomb where he was buried. They missed Jesus very much and were very sad. But when they reached the tomb, the big stone at the entrance was rolled away. Jesus's body wasn't there! Instead, they found angels, who told the women, "Jesus is not here! He is risen!"

The women were so happy to hear this news that they ran to tell the rest of the disciples.

LOOK-AND-FIND

1 one big stone

2 two greeting angels

3 three jars of spices

4 four flying birds

5 five fluffy clouds

6 six wiggly worms

7 seven fluttering butterflies

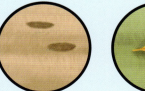
8 eight dusty footprints

9 nine little leaves

10 ten flowering lilies

JESUS IS RISEN!

Most of the disciples didn't believe what the angels had said. Was Jesus really alive again? Peter and John ran to see where Jesus had been buried. They found that the tomb was empty, just as the women told them!

Mary Magdalene had heard what the angels said, but she was still worried about where Jesus could be. What if someone had stolen his body? She stayed in the garden, crying, and a man who Mary thought was a gardener came to comfort her. "Mary, why are you crying? I am alive!" It wasn't a gardener—it was Jesus!

LOOK-AND-FIND

1 one risen Jesus

2 two racing disciples

3 three burial cloths

4 four gardening tools

5 five bundles of flowers

6 six sprinting squirrels

7 seven dangling vines

8 eight fallen fruits

9 nine munching caterpillars

10 ten pink blossoms

JESUS APPEARS TO THE DISCIPLES

After Jesus died, many of them decided to hide from the people who had killed him. The disciples thought maybe the soldiers would try to hurt them too, so they locked themselves in one of their homes. But suddenly, something amazing happened—Jesus appeared! "Peace be with you," he said to them. The disciples could see the scars on his hands and feet and knew it was really him. They were so happy to see Jesus again!

LOOK-AND-FIND

1 one locked door

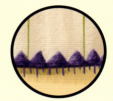
2 two woven tapestries

3 three sneaky mice

4 four colorful rugs

5 five baskets of food

6 six closed curtains

7 seven glowing lamps

8 eight floor cushions

9 nine potted plants

10 ten hiding disciples

ROAD TO EMMAUS

On their journey to a town called Emmaus, two people were talking about how much they missed Jesus. They were very sad he had died. When a stranger joined them on the road, he asked, "Who are you talking about?"

The two travelers invited the man to stop and eat with them so they could tell him all about Jesus. The stranger blessed the bread and broke it—and then disappeared! They realized *he* was Jesus!

The two travelers were so excited! It was true—Jesus was alive!

LOOK-AND-FIND

1 one traveling stranger

2 two walking sticks

3 three dinner plates

4 four hiking gazelles

5 five tall trees

6 six weaving spiders

7 seven roadside rocks

8 eight tufts of grass

9 nine pieces of firewood

10 ten bright poppies

BREAKFAST WITH JESUS

On the sea of Galilee, the disciples were having a bad night of fishing: their nets were completely empty. Early in the morning, someone called to them from the shore. He told them to try casting the net on the other side of their boat. Would that make a difference? But when the disciples did so and then pulled up their net, it was full of fish!

"It is the Lord!" Peter shouted. He jumped out of the boat and swam to meet Jesus. "Come and have breakfast," Jesus invited, and they all ate bread and fish together.

LOOK-AND-FIND

1 one swimming Peter

2 two rolling barrels

3 three sweating disciples

4 four palm trees

5 five hideaway crabs

6 six stray ropes

7 seven flopping fish

8 eight pieces of stuck seaweed

9 nine surveying gulls

10 ten choppy waves

JESUS ASCENDS

One day, the disciples met Jesus on a hilltop in Galilee. When everyone arrived, he said, "God has given me all authority in heaven and on earth. Go and make disciples of all nations, baptize them, and teach them everything I taught you." After he said this, Jesus rose up into the clouds until the disciples could no longer see him.

Angels appeared. "Jesus is in heaven," they said, "but someday he will come back the same way you saw him go. In the meantime, the Holy Spirit will guide you." The disciples were filled with joy. They hurried home and began to tell everyone about Jesus. Some traveled the world and others wrote down stories about him. And now we know about Jesus too!

LOOK-AND-FIND

1 one ascending Jesus

2 two happy angels

3 three traveling donkeys

4 four gospel writers

5 five cheering children

6 six hurrying disciples

7 seven billowing clouds

8 eight olive trees

9 nine faraway homes

10 ten yellow flowers

Copyright © 2025 Beaming Books. All rights reserved.

No part of this book may be reproduced without the written permission of the publisher.

Email copyright@beamingbooks.com

30 29 28 27 26 25 24   1 2 3 4 5 6 7 8

Hardcover ISBN: 979-8-8898-3483-0

eBook ISBN: 979-8-8898-3484-7

Library of Congress Control Number: 2024943646 (print)

Beaming Books
PO Box 1209
Minneapolis, MN 55440-1209

Printed in China.